Big Machines

BULLDOZERS

By Katie Kawa

Gareth Stevens
Publishing

Please visit our website, www.garethstevens.com. For a free color catalog of all our high-quality books, call toll free 1-800-542-2595 or fax 1-877-542-2596.

Library of Congress Cataloging-in-Publication Data

Kawa, Katie.
Bulldozers / Katie Kawa.
     p. cm. — (Big machines)
Includes index.
ISBN 978-1-4339-5552-5 (pbk.)
ISBN 978-1-4339-5553-2 (6-pack)
ISBN 978-1-4339-5550-1 (library binding)
1. Bulldozers—Juvenile literature. I. Title.
TA725.K335 2011
629.225—dc22
                                    2011006537

First Edition

Published in 2012 by
Gareth Stevens Publishing
111 East 14th Street, Suite 349
New York, NY 10003

Copyright © 2012 Gareth Stevens Publishing

Editor: Katie Kawa
Designer: Daniel Hosek

Photo credits: Cover, pp. 1, 5, 7, 9, 11, 13, 15, 19, 23 Shutterstock.com; p. 17 James P. Blair/ National Geographic/Getty Images; p. 21 Thinkstock.com.

Printed in the United States of America

CPSIA compliance information: Batch #CS11GS: For further information contact Gareth Stevens, New York, New York at 1-800-542-2595.

Contents

Bulldozers are strong!

They move things. They move by pushing.

7

They use a tool to push.
It is called a blade.

The blade is on the front of the bulldozer.

The blade is made of metal. It is sharp!

They dig dirt! They use a ripper to dig deep.

15

Bulldozers move lots of things. They move big trees!

They make roads.
They take away rocks
and dirt.

19

They work in the city.
They help make new
buildings.

21

They work on farms. They clear land for plants.

Words to Know

blade

ripper

Index